UN Peace Operations

Part VI

Challenges of Mission Leadership in UN Peace Operations in delivering the mandate

UN Peace Operations

Part VI

Challenges of Mission Leadership in UN Peace Operations in delivering the mandate

Edited by

A K Bardalai and Pradeep Goswami

(Established 1870)

A Joint USI - ICWA Publication

Vij Books India Pvt Ltd
New Delhi (India)

Published by

Vij Books India Pvt Ltd
(Publishers, Distributors & Importers)
2/19, Ansari Road
Delhi – 110 002
Phones: 91-11-43596460
Mob: 98110 94883
e-mail: contact@vijpublishing.com
web : www.vijbooks.in

First Published in India in 2022

ISBN: 978-93-93499-13-4

Contents

Preface

In the year 2021, The United Services Institution (USI) of India, a leading independent think tank of India, with support from the Indian Council of World Affairs (ICWA), planned and conducted a series of webinars on UN peace operations under:

(a) **27 February 2021**. India and UN Peace Operations: Principles of UN Peacekeeping and Mandates (https://usiofindia.org/wp-content/uploads/2022/01/Monograph-Principals-of-Peacekeeping-Mandate.pdf).

(b) **29 June 2021**. UN Peace Operations: Hostage-taking of UN Peacekeepers (https://usiofindia.org/wp-content/uploads/2022/01/Monograph_Hostage-Taking-of-Peacekeepers.pdf).

(c) **25 August 2021**. Effectiveness of UN Peace Operations: Dynamics of Composition of Troops and Diversity of UN Peace Operations (https://usiofindia.org/wp-content/uploads/2022/01/UN-Monograph-Part-III-Effectiveness.pdf).

(d) **22 October 2021**. UN Peace Operations: Protection of Civilians (https://usiofindia.org/wp-content/uploads/2022/01/UN-Peacekeeping-Part-IV_-PoC.pdf)

(e) **09 Feb 2022.** UN Peace Operations: Women, Peace & Security. (https://usiofindia.org/wp-content/uploads/2022/06/UN-Peace-Operations-Part-V-Women-Peace-and-Security.pdf)

(f) **21 April 2022.** UN Peace Operations: Challenges of Mission Leadership in UN Peace Operations in delivering the mandate.

The peace operations landscape has evolved dramatically since the first UN Peacekeeping Mission. Keeping and sustaining peace has, over the past decade, arguably become more dangerous. Added to this are the significant policy shifts during the last decade to address changing environment, like the Sustaining Peace Agenda, which emphasises the whole spectrum of conflict prevention, peace operations, and peacebuilding; the reaffirmation of key policies such as the protection of civilians and the Women, Peace, and Security Agenda; and the emergence of new normative frameworks such as the Youth, Peace and Security Agenda.

One recurring theme in these policy shifts has been the reiteration of the importance of effective, courageous, and accountable leadership in UN peace operations. This subject, and its associated challenges have been fundamental to the reviews of UN peace operations and an instrumental aspect in the ongoing UN system reforms. Thus, when it comes to UN mission leadership, good is not good enough. However, there are several tangible and intangible factors that affect mission leadership. We will be addressing these issues in today's webinar.

To understand the challenges of UN mission leadership in delivering mandate, the perspective of four former peacekeepers who served in earlier missions and one UN civilian staff member currently serving as one of the senior mission leaders of one of the current missions will highlight the challenges.

This monograph is a compilation of talks by eminent speakers during the webinar on "UN Peace Operations: Challenges of Mission Leadership in UN Peace Operations in delivering the mandate".

About the Participants

Major General BK Sharma, AVSM, SM (Retd)** is the Director of the USI of India, India's oldest think tank established by the British in 1870. He has tenanted prestigious assignments in India, including command of a mountain division on the China border and Senior Faculty Member at the National Defence College, New Delhi. He has represented his country at the UN as Military Observer in Central America and has been India's Defence Attaché in Central Asia. He specialises in Strategic Net Assessment methodology, Scenario Building, and Strategic Gaming.

Ambassador Vijay Thakur Singh is the Director General (DG), ICWA, a premium think tank of the Ministry of External Affairs. She is a carrier diplomat and had multilateral experience during her service with the Ministry of External Affairs, GOI. She was High Commissioner of India to Singapore and Ireland and prior to that, Joint Secretary to the President of India and Joint Secretary at the National Security Council Secretariat (NSCS). She also handled Afghanistan and Pakistan desk in the Ministry of External Affairs and was Counsellor at the Embassy of India in Kabul. She was also a Counsellor in the Permanent Mission of India to the United Nations in New York. She retired in September 2020 as Secretary (East), Ministry of External Affairs.

Major General PK Goswami, VSM (Retd) is the Deputy Director at the USI of India and Head of the USI UN Cell. He is also the chief coordinator for a series of USI – ICWA webinars on UN Peace Operations. He was a Military Observer with

United Nations Verification Mission at Angola (UNAVEM) from 1991 to 1992 and Senior Faculty at National Defence College, New Delhi. He represented National Defence College, India, at the 16th ASEAN Regional Forum for Heads of Defence Universities, Colleges, and Institutions in Beijing, China, in November 2012.

Lieutenant General Chander Prakash, SM, VSM (Retd) is a veteran of the Indian Army and has held a number of important military command and staff appointments at various levels both in India and abroad. He was Indian Defence Advisor in France from 2005 to 2008, the Senior Sector Operations Officer in the United Nations Iran-Iraq Military Observers Group, on the Board of Management at Centre for UN Peacekeeping (CUNPK), New Delhi, and later Force Commander of UN Peacekeeping Mission in the Democratic Republic of Congo (MONUSCO) from August 2010 to March 2013. Post-retirement from active service in the army, he served as the Deputy Director and Editor at USI of India, New Delhi.

Lieutenant General Satish Nambiar, PVSM, AVSM, VrC (Retd) is a veteran of the 1965 and 1971 wars and has served the Indian Army within India and abroad and is a former Director of the USI of India. He was the first Force Commander and Head of Mission of the United Nations forces in the former Yugoslavia (UNPROFOR). During his tenure as the Director of USI, he was appointed as Adviser to the Government of Sri Lanka on the peace process in that country from 2002 to 2003 and was a member of the UN 16 member high-level panel to study global security threats and recommend measures for effective collective action. The General is the recipient of the Indian national award of Padma Bhushan for his contribution to national security affairs.

Lieutenant General JS Lidder, UYSM, AVSM (Retd) is a veteran of the 1971 war, served the Indian Army for over 40 years, and has held a number of important military command and staff appointments at various levels both in India and abroad. He has vast UN experience in both political and military spheres. He was Chief of Staff in ONUMOZ (Mozambique) from 1994-95 and Force Commander UNMIS (Sudan) from 2005-08. Post military retirement, he was Deputy SRSG UNMIS from 2010-11. As senior-most UN diplomat based at Jumba, he led the UN efforts for conflict resolution and peacebuilding. Most importantly South Sudan Referendum led to the birth of the new nation in July 2011. Presently he is involved with multiple UN Offices, global think tanks, and training establishments as an expert and mentor.

Mr Jack Christofides, a former South African diplomate, is currently the Deputy Head of Mission and Director of Political and Civil Affairs of UNIFIL since March 2020. Earlier, he was the Director of the Northern Africa Division of the Departments of Political and Peacebuilding Affairs (DPPA) and Peace Operations (DPO), Director of the Africa II Division of the Office of Operations in the Department of Peacekeeping Operations (DPKO), the Director for the Division of Policy, Evaluation and Training in DPKO and the Department of Field Support (DFS), Team Leader for Sudan and the Great Lakes. In addition, he has extensive field experience at various levels of the UN and was also stationed in Geneva covering human rights issues, first as a diplomat and then as Chief of Staff to the United Nations High Commissioner for Human Rights.

Lieutenant General SS Tinaikar, SM, VSM (Retd) is a veteran of the elite Parachute Regiment of the Indian Army and has held several important military command and staff appointments at various levels both in India and abroad. He has rich experience working in United Nations Peacekeeping Operations, being a Military Observer in UNAVEM-III and Chief Operations Officer in UNMIS; before being appointed as Force Commander UNMISS from June 2019 to January 2022.

Concept Note

UN Peace Operations: Challenges of Mission Leadership in Delivering the Mandate

The mission leadership in UN peace operations has a crucial role to play in operationalizing and helping in achieving a given mandate to the mission by the UNSC. The UN peace operations are multi-faceted, with the military component playing a crucial role in terms of providing a secure environment and protecting of civilians. The senior mission leadership of which the political head is the Special Representative of the Secretary-General (SRSG) and the military head, the Force Commander (FC), has enviable tasks to perform primarily for two reasons. *One*, the decision-making process in the ever-evolving politico-military environment is highly complex and challenging. *Two*, even though the Head of the Mission (HoM), usually a civilian, draws his authority from the Secretary-General based on the UN charter, wherein the directives and guidelines are broad-based, and interpretations vary.

The Force Commander faces increasing challenges in the violent operating environment to operationalize the given mandate, namely force deployment, its management, and ensuring optimal performance by all military contingents. Military contingents of a mission are from diverse backgrounds, lack interoperability, and are often reluctant to follow the laid down UN policy on *Command and Control* of peacekeeping missions. It is, therefore, up to the HoM (and the FC) to work around such constraints and find ways to exercise his/their authority. In effect, FC's, 'command and control' function implies the dynamic deployment of the force and its proactive employment. The diversity among the contingents in terms of training, equipment, and varied perceptions of peacekeeping and mandate are challenges mission leaders face on a regular basis while implementing the mandate. The employment of the uniformed peacekeepers is dictated by the prevailing circumstances as well as the ingenuity of the mission leadership. Under such circumstances, leadership traits include the ability to adapt to transforming conflicts and take risks for the effectiveness of peace operations.

In integrated UN peacekeeping missions, the SRSG is the highest political leader in the missions and is expected to play a coordinating role within as well as outside the UN, while complimentary roles are performed by the FC when it comes to matters military. The mission leaders have to navigate unchartered waters and operate between conflicting interests while still adhering to the norms and principles of peacekeeping and delivering impartial resolutions in the mission area. Besides, because of the inherent ambiguity in the interpretation of certain UN norms, especially the principles of peacekeeping, when it comes to making critical decisions, a leader (both political and military), generally tend to interpret the mandate in terms of the mission (at time personal) gain/loss of prestige. While some leaders may be willing to suffer the loss of prestige for a benevolent decision taken, other leaders may go the extra mile when it comes to saving lives. The massacre of Bosnian Muslims in Srebrenica in July 1995 and the genocide in Rwanda in April 1994 are a few such examples. But there are also opposite examples of the UN Stabilization Mission in Haiti (MINUSTAH) in 2005 and Cote d'Ivoire in April 2011.

Besides the uniformed peacekeepers, there is a substantial number of civilian components (both UN and local), who have their mandate regarding the humanitarian tasks and also provide support to the mission's overall operations. While the department of political and peacebuilding affairs (UN DPPA) provides political advice to the leaders, those from the mission support provide the logistic support for the operational activities.

Modern UN operations are multi-dimensional and undertake multiple mandated tasks by deploying an array of enabling agencies, department resources, and uniformed personnel in a mission area. Most missions have the field staff of the Office of the UN High Commissioner for Refugees, the World Food Program, the UN Children's Fund, the Office for the Coordination of Humanitarian Affairs, the UN Development Program, and the Office of the UN High Commissioner for Human Rights. Besides these well-recognized offices, civil affairs, coordinators in Women Peace and Security, Child Protection teams, and Justice and Corrections Section may also be working closely with each other.

Peacekeepers at times have also been called upon to support the activities of international or local non-governmental organizations engaged in providing humanitarian assistance to victims of conflicts. The ability of the mission to implement the mandate, therefore, depends on the coordinated and synergized actions of all these elements, which have their own challenges, interests, and mandates. However, diversity amongst the peacekeeping contingents and different work ethos of the civilian staff tend to pull the mission in different directions, at times away from the mission's overall goals. It becomes more complicated in a complex intra-state conflicts like CAR, DRC, and South Sudan where violent intra-party/armed groups clashes make the innocent populations suffer. The peacekeepers also become a target of violence, and some may also compromise the status the impartiality, legitimacy, and credibility because of a mission-state relationship. Under such circumstances, it is the individual leadership characteristics that can be the sole turning point in the trajectory of peace operations.

This webinar intends to discuss the Challenges of Mission Leadership in UN Peace Operations in delivering the mandate. It would address the following questions:

(a) Since the mandate is a product of political compromises of the Security Council, how does it affect the mission in setting its goal?

(b) Among other factors, the success of the peace operation depends on the contribution of both civilian and military components of the mission. However, since the relationship between the military and civilian components is most tenuous, how do the HoM and FC navigate to get the best out of these components for a better mission performance?

(c) Many TCCs tend to take advantage of the ambiguity in the UN norms and interpret the definitions of the principles of peacekeeping to suit their own interests. Different and ambiguous interpretation of the principles is likely to adversely affect the performance of the peace operations, especially when it comes to a mandate like 'protection of civilian (PoC)'. How can the HoM and the FC contribute to minimizing the adverse impact of the ambiguity?

(d) Diversity among the uniformed peacekeeping contingents and between the contingents and the civilian components works against the operational efficiency of the mission. At the level of HoM and FC, how best this diversity can be turned into an advantage to achieve a mission's goals?

(e) Adherence to the principles of peacekeeping provides legitimacy and credibility. But when the host state or its government forces are complicit in the crimes against its population, how does the mission-host state relationship impact mandate implementation while respecting sovereign sensitivity?

(f) PoC is one of the core goals of modern peace operations. For PoC, the available tools like the security sector, and judicial and structural reforms are the long-term peace-building measures. The UN POC Policy of 2019 tries to bridge the theory-practice gap. At times the peacekeepers are outstretched in providing immediate physical protection. On the other hand, when the peacekeepers provide physical protection, the mission gets visibility, and credibility and earns cooperation from the local population. But when the host state itself is complicit in the violence against its own population and is averse to immediate reforms, how can the leadership operationalize the PoC mandate while keeping the Human Rights Due Diligence Policy (HRDDP) in mind?

(g) Centre of gravity for any successful peace operation lies with the local population. UN peace operations will always get local legitimacy based on their impact on and evaluation by the local population. Strategic communication i.e., the ability of the mission to communicate correctly with the population plays a crucial role in it. Given the diversity within the mission, how do strategize communication as a part of the overall vision of the mission and manage expectations?

The webinar will aim to find answers to the above questions from the participants:

(a) Perspective of a former HoM and FC of UNPROFOR.

(b) Perspective of a former FC and Deputy SRSG (Deputy HoM) of UNMISS.

(c) Perspective of Dy HoM and Director of Political and Civil Affairs of UNIFIL.

(d) Special remarks by a former FC of UNMISS.

Introductory Remarks

Maj Gen PK Goswami, VSM (Retd)

On behalf of Maj Gen BK Sharma, Director, USI and Amb Vijay Thakur Singh, Director General, ICWA, I welcome all participants to today's webinar.

I am glad to inform all that since 2021, the USI, in collaboration with ICWA, is conducting a series of webinars on UN-related issues. The inaugural webinar was held on 27 Feb 2021 on 'Principles of UN Peace Keeping and Mandate', followed by 'The Impact of Climate Change on UN Peacekeeping Operations' on 20 Apr 2021 in collaboration with NUPI & SIPRI, 'UN Peace Operations: Hostage-taking of UN Peacekeepers' on 29 June 21, 'Effectiveness of UN Peace Operations' with focus on 'Dynamics of Composition of Troops and Diversity on UN Peace Operations' on 25 Aug 2021, UN Peace Operations: Protection of Civilians on 21 Oct 2022, and on 'UN Peace Operations: Women, Peace, and Security on 09 Feb 2022.

At the conclusion of each webinar, all talks are being compiled and printed as a Monograph, to share the rich experience of speakers, with a larger audience and cross-fertilization of ideas.

Today is the sixth one, and we will deliberate on **'UN Peace Operations: Challenges of Mission Leadership in Delivering the Mandate'.**

I express my deep gratitude to Jack Christofides, currently the Deputy Head of Mission and Director of Political and Civil Affairs of UNIFIL Lebanon, Lieutenant General Nambiar, first Force Commander and Head of Mission of the United Nations forces in the former Yugoslavia (UNPROFOR), Lieutenant General Lidder, former Chief of Staff in ONUMOZ (Mozambique), Force Commander UNMIS (Sudan) and then Deputy SRSG UNMIS, Lieutenant General Chander Prakash, former Force Commander of UN Peacekeeping Mission in the Democratic Republic of Congo (MONUSCO), and Lieutenant General Tinaikar, former Military Observer in UNAVEM-III, Chief Operations Officer in UNMIS and later Force Commander UNMISS, for accepting my request to share their rich experience and deep insight on Challenges of the Mission Leadership. They will be introduced by the moderator as we proceed further with the webinar. We are also fortunate to have a galaxy of UN professionals and practitioners and friends from Turkey, Bangladesh, Nepal, Sri Lanka, and S Korea participating in the event today.

Major General BK Sharma, AVSM, SM** (Retd) is the Director of the USI of India. He has tenanted prestigious assignments in India, including command of a mountain division on the China border and Senior Faculty Member at the National Defence College, New Delhi. He has represented his country at the UN as Military Observer in Central America and has been India's Defence Attaché in Central Asia. He specialises in Strategic Net Assessment methodology, Scenario Building and Strategic Gaming. Now Major General BK Sharma, Director, USI of India, will deliver his Opening Remarks.

To discuss today's theme, we have past and present UN Mission Leaders, who are practitioners and have in-depth knowledge of UN peace operations and have written extensively. Of all the five speakers, their opinions may vary, but I believe that at the end of the discussions, our takeaways will help us better clarify the subject. Therefore, to begin the proceedings, we have someone who has got an insight into the UN Mission leadership, having been head of the UN mission, Congo from 2010 to 2013.

Our moderator for the event today is Lieutenant General Chander Prakash, a veteran of the Indian Army who has held several important military command and staff appointments at various levels both in India and abroad. He was Indian Defence Advisor in France from 2005 to 2008, the Senior Sector Operations Officer in the United Nations Iran-Iraq Military Observers Group, on the Board of Management at Centre for UN Peacekeeping (CUNPK), New Delhi and later Force Commander of UN Peacekeeping Mission in the Democratic Republic of Congo (MONUSCO) from August 2010 to March 2013. Post-retirement from active service in the army, he served as the Deputy Director and Editor at USI of India, New Delhi.

Opening Address

*Maj Gen BK Sharma, AVSM, SM** (Retd)*

Thank you Major General Pradeep Goswami. At the outset, I am immensely pleased to extend a hearty welcome to Ambassador Vijay Thakur Singh and other esteemed panellists, particularly Lt General Satish Nambiar who is the father of the UN Peacekeeping Center in India and has also been the global expert on UN peacekeeping. What gives me added happiness is that he has been our director and most of the other eminent panellists here for example Lt General Chander Prakash has been the Deputy Director & Editor at the USI. Similarly, Lt General JS Lidder is a life member and so is Major General AK Bardalai who was earlier a Senior Research Fellow and is presently a Distinguished Fellow at the USI.

As we see the panellists have served in some of the most difficult mission areas at the topmost positions and therefore they have a wealth of knowledge to share with us today. We would spend more time listening to them and absorbing their experiences about this particular subject. But just to make a customary introductory remark, I would say that the UN missions today have become highly multi-dimensional with a host of UN departments, human rights organizations, and agencies dealing with child and women protection all enmeshed together. The military contingents are drawn from various group contributing countries with varying ethos, beliefs, cultures, priorities and their own interpretation of the UN mandate, depending on their respective national interests. Mission leaders are expected to deliver in an alien kind of a conflict environment which is marked by sectarian violence and ethnic conflicts.

Most of the mission areas are in the throes of very complex conflicts; the lines between the role of state actors and non-state actors, which keep ever interchanging, have become very blurred. This entire environment is characterized by volatility, uncertainty, complexity and ambiguity. We often see unforeseen eventualities erupt and conflict scenarios demand robust and flexible responses and deployment of more resources, which are not always available. When unexpected situations put mission leaders and the peacekeepers on the horns of a dilemma, UN peace operations often come under media glare. HIPPO report has very aptly summarized the challenges of today's senior military leadership as being in an environment where demands and responsibilities are not matched with adequate preparation and capacity building. There are always tensions between the Secretary General's authority and member states in regard to the selection and appointment of senior military mission leaders.

There are other areas such as a lack of consistent application of the existing merit-based selection process, and the challenge of finding candidates with both political and military skills or managerial skills. Other issues are that of gender and geographical representation, poor induction and continued support for newly appointed senior mission leaders. Another area that has been identified is the failure to grow the capacity of those with weak leadership potential. You cannot learn on the job - it's very difficult once you're in the quagmire of a situation, you cannot start doing on-the-job training. Therefore, our focus today is on how we select, groom, train, ensure high performance, and fix accountability of these mission leaders.

When I go back to my own experience with the UN, I saw this multi-dimensional environment in the Central American Republics, where we were involved in the disarming and demobilization of the Contras rebels. Our mission area actually encompassed all the five states because some of these Contras were being supported from the bases of other countries, and there was a major power that was involved in supporting Contras against the Sandinistas (Nicaragua). I have seen from a very close quarter this complexity. Imagine if tomorrow a mission is to be deployed in Afghanistan which is facing an unprecedented humanitarian crisis. It will be a very different mandate with a multitude of agencies acting in tandem. Therefore it is high time that we start drawing lessons from some of these complex missions, based on the experience of our mission leaders there, and try and factor them in our entire process of selection, grooming and accountability of mission leaders.

Our mission leader ought to be conversant with geopolitics, and have an understanding of the strategic-security environment, the cultural map of mission areas, international treaties and similar issues. So I think there is a requirement for a *de novo* look at leadership selection and grooming to produce effective mission leaders for the evolving UNPK missions.

Challenges of Mission Leadership: Perspective of a former HoM and FC of UNPROFOR

Lt Gen Satish Nambiar, PVSM, AVSM, VrC (Retd)

It is indeed a pleasure and a privilege to participate in the event this afternoon organised by the United Service Institution of India and the Indian Council of World Affairs, both of which institutions I have had a long and rewarding association, within the years past.

In the next twenty minutes or so, I shall try and share with you some of my experiences as the First Force Commander and Head of the UN Peacekeeping Mission in the former Yugoslavia in 1992/93 in the context of the subject of this afternoon's webinar. Let me start with a few words on the components of the Mission I had the honour and privilege of setting up, and the composition of the senior mission leadership, as both aspects have a significant bearing on the subject under discussion. UNPROFOR was set up by the UN Security Council under the authority of a Resolution adopted on 15 February 1992 and was, at that time, the largest peacekeeping mission undertaken by the United Nations in Europe at that, all the media focus was consequently generated. The Mission was mandated to deploy in four delineated areas within Croatia that were Serb-dominated and where fighting had taken place before an agreement was reached for UN deployment. These areas were designated as

United Nations Protected Areas (UNPAs) - one contiguous to Serbia, and the other three to Bosnia-Herzegovina (BiH). As the Mission started deployment for its mandated task in Croatia, with the ill-conceived direction of setting up headquarters in Sarajevo (the capital of BiH), political developments like the secession by BiH from the Federal Republic of Yugoslavia (FRY), and the consequent fighting between the three communities (Muslims about 45 %, Serbs about 37 % and about 10% Croats) resulted in UNPROFOR being flooded with mandates by the UN Security Council for actions within BiH, primarily for assistance in humanitarian action, and in due course, to prevent fighting between the warring parties. Therefore, whereas the Mission strength started with a little over 14,000 personnel for the initially mandated mission within Croatia, it went up to over 28,000 by the time I left on 2nd March 1993 after exactly a year at the helm, with mandated deployments within Bosnia-Herzegovina, and later even in Macedonia.

The first point I may make with some emphasis is that UNPROFOR was the first peacekeeping mission, and possibly the last, to have significant contributions from four of the five permanent members of the Security Council. There was a very strong French contribution (with two infantry battalions and a logistics battalion); a Russian contingent of an infantry battalion; the British initially made a medical contribution that was pulled out, and subsequently, a battalion contingent was provided for deployment in BiH; about six months into the mission, the USA provided a field hospital located at the Zagreb airport. There were also staff officers, military observers, civilian police, and administrative personnel from these countries.

Battalion/Regiment-sized contributions were provided by several developed countries like Belgium, Canada (two infantry battalions and an engineer battalion), Denmark,

Finland, Sweden (personnel for my headquarters staff and an infantry battalion), Norway, and Spain.

Erstwhile Warsaw Pact countries like Czechoslovakia, Poland, and later Ukraine provided battalion-sized contingents. As things transpired, Czechoslovakia underwent a political split during that period, but the battalion remained a single entity under my command, at least till I left.

From the developing world, I had battalion-sized contingents from Argentina, Egypt, Jordan, Kenya, Nepal and Nigeria. In addition, staff officers for my headquarters and sub-ordinate headquarters, a large complement of UNMOs, and civilian police personnel were provided by these countries as also, as many more.

By the time I relinquished the charge on completion of my one-year contract, I had uniformed personnel from about 34 countries of the world under my command and civilian staff from many more. A unique experience. Hence, I look back at the assignment with a sense of great satisfaction and fulfilment.

It is of course, another matter altogether that I had no Indian troops or police personnel under my command, as the Government of India had, in their wisdom, taken a decision not to contribute. I, therefore, went in to meet the challenge with one personal staff officer (of my choice).

I was the Director-General of Military Operations at that time and was deputed at seven days' notice to report at UN HQ in New York on 2nd March 1992. The selection and nomination of the staff officer who accompanied me have their own lessons in terms of senior military leadership decision-making capability. Due to paucity of time, I homed in on one of the officers from the Mechanised Infantry Regiment, of which I was then the Colonel (an assignment

I took over from its founder General K Sundarji on his superannuation on 31 May 1988). I had been impressed by Major Philip Campose during one of my visits to formations and units and picked on him as he was in New Delhi in the Military Secretary's Branch. I called him on the telephone to ask him whether he was prepared to accompany me. The only request he made was that he be allowed to check with his newly wedded wife before responding. Within a short while, he confirmed his willingness to go with me. But there was a twist to the tale – that his boss (a couple of levels above - the Additional Military Secretary) was not prepared to spare him, indispensable as he was to the functioning of the Indian Army. I told him I would revert to him and called up the Military Secretary, Lt Gen R Narasimhan (a couple of years senior to me in age and in Service, from whom I had taken over the Division we both commanded), and told him my problem. The response was spontaneous and truly episodical and will stay with me till my dying day. He said "Satish, if the Chief of the Army Staff can spare his Director General of Military Operations for the Mission, how dare the Military Secretary decline to provide a Major from his staff? Philip Campose will go with you". And the rest, as they say, is history. I am proud that the choice I made was also in many ways, an indication of the ability of senior military commanders to recognize professional competence and talent. Philip Campose served me well and retired as the Vice Chief of the Army Staff a few years ago.

A few words on the set of meetings and briefings in New York prior to departure for Belgrade on 8th March 1992, are of significance. At my meeting with the Secretary-General Boutrous Boutrous Ghali, he clearly warned me that the mission would be tough and demanding, as there would inevitably be attempts by the Europeans and the USA to try and influence activities. He however assured me that I could depend on full and unqualified support from him and his staff at the UN HQ. Which I must say was forthcoming in full measure and without any reservations whatsoever right through my assignment. The major players were - the Under Secretary-General DPKO Marrack Goulding (from the UK), Assistant Secretary-General Kofi Annan (from Ghana), who took over as Under-Secretary-General DPKO from Goulding in February 1993, with both of whom I developed a rewarding and enduring relationship based on mutual respect and understanding. I also had the pleasure of meeting for the first time and getting to know well in due course, Shashi Tharoor, who was initially Executive Assistant to Marrack Goulding and then with Kofi Annan. Such understanding with the hierarchy at UN HQ, and mutual recognition and acknowledgement of one another's professional competence, is vital for effective senior mission leadership. It must be built up from the start.

The first contact I had with my senior mission colleagues (the 'Command Group' as it were), was at a briefing on 4th March 1992 at the UN HQ in New York, where we had all been thoughtfully assembled by DPKO – Deputy Force Commander, Major General Phillipe Morillon (France); Director Civil Affairs Cedric Thornberry (Irish, from the UN Secretariat); Chief of Staff, Brigadier Lewis McKenzie (Canada); Chief Military Observer, Brigadier John Wilson (Australia); Chief Operations Observer, Colonel Svend Harders (Denmark); Chief Administrative Officer (USA); Sector Commanders at the rank of Brigadier/Senior Colonel, from Argentina, Kenya, Nigeria & Russia; and Police Commissioner from Norway. All proven professionals.

When I first addressed them, I could sense they were assessing me. Is this guy competent enough to exercise command over us, and provide effective leadership for the successful conduct of the mission mandate? To their eternal credit, I must state that, within a couple of weeks into the Mission, when I had shown them through my professional competence and leadership skills acquired in the Indian Army over three and a half decades, handling the local leadership of the parties to the conflict, command of the language of the Mission (English), handling of the media, and the rapport I was able to establish with the subordinate staff and personnel of the HQ and the units, that I was as good, if not better than any of them, their response was absolutely unreserved, without exception. That was one of the most gratifying and enduring features of my command tenure. It showed that professional competence and leadership qualities have no national or racial connotations. They are recognised for what they are.

In the process of effecting the deployment and tasking of the various contingents and framing the Rules of Engagement (ROE) for the mission, I learnt and mastered the art of what I now term "Consultative Leadership". A most useful form of exercising leadership, particularly in such international commitments paid great dividends, as my colleagues had a sense of participation and ownership of the decisions that were arrived at. Needless to say, where it was not possible to arrive at a consensus, the final decision was clearly mine, in the knowledge that the final responsibility rested on my shoulders. And accepted as such without any reservations.

From the very outset, it was made quite clear that I would make no compromises insofar as the conduct of the activities of the Mission was concerned. And to highlight this aspect I may mention that within a few months of the setting up of the mission I initiated and arranged for the replacement of two very senior members of my Command Group; both as it happened, from P5 member states. This was managed with some finesse and without drawing undue attention, through the assistance of the SG and USG DPKO, with the understanding and cooperation of the affected member state representatives at UN HQ. I make this point to stress that such actions, even if unpleasant, are necessary. Not only for the effective conduct of the Mission but to convey to all, that incompetence and lethargy are just not acceptable.

A most desirable but rarely mentioned quality in senior leaders (particularly military), is a sense of humour. It served me well through the various stages of my journey in the Indian Army. And I put it to great effect in command of UNPROFOR. In fact, it got me through many trying situations, including in my interaction with the leadership of the warring parties, and the media, and made a great impression on my command.

Let me now turn to some of the major problems that arise in the conduct of mission activities and have to be handled by the senior mission leadership with proper understanding, imagination, finesse and perseverance.

The first is the perennial problem not only of lack of political support from some of the major powers, including those that were party to the setting up of the Mission but on many occasions, the manipulation that is indulged in at the local level in dissonance with the mandate of the Mission. The sad irony is that while I mention this as a problem, I was faced with thirty years ago, by the accounts one hears even today, it still apparently persists. In my case, the great personal rapport I had established with Cyrus Vance (former US Secretary of State, and the UN SG's Special Envoy at the Geneva-based European Conference on the former Yugoslavia), and Lord David Owen (former Foreign Secretary of the UK and the EU representative at the Conference), and the full support I received from the senior staff at UN HQ, saw me through. Hence the only piece of advice I can offer those of you who have to deal with the problem is, to manage to get some of the powerful guys on your side from the start.

The second and equally demanding problem is that of dealing with the local leadership. I was doing so at the top levels, with the Presidents of the Federal Republic of Yugoslavia (FRY), Croatia, and later BiH and Macedonia. From my own experience, I can state quite unequivocally, we should have no doubts that these interlocutors, no matter what the level, will manipulate, cheat, lie, and dishonour agreements (even written ones), without batting an eyelid. Hence that aspect must be factored into your responses, reactions, and implementation measures.

The third problem and one that has been highlighted in the Concept Paper, is of diverse training standards and equipment availability. It is futile to bemoan this aspect because, given the manner in which the peacekeeping commitment is handled by the UN, such diversity is inevitable; even so, it is not an insurmountable problem. Training aspects are being effectively addressed by activities run by organisations like our Centre for United Nations Peacekeeping (CUNPK) but will remain. But non-availability of 'state of the art' equipment for UNPKO will remain a handicap for as long as the developed world, which has the wherewithal both in terms of trained manpower and equipment, remains detached from the activity. Mission leadership has to work through the problem through appropriate tasking and implementation.

The fourth perennial problem is the military-civilian interface in the mission. It is a sad reflection on the state of affairs that in command of UNPROFOR in the initial stages, I had to spend almost 20% of my time (that could have been otherwise more usefully applied) in resolving this problem. To the great credit of my senior colleagues, however, both military and international civilian staff, we kept it at manageable levels with some deft handling and did not allow it to impact the effective conduct of Mission activities. Needless to say, I am somewhat disappointed that 30 years down the line, the problem still apparently persists. Personally, I think it has much to do with the UN bureaucracy that merits a radical overhaul.

In addition to the aspect of political machinations mentioned earlier in the context of problem number 1, in most major missions there is invariably scope for, and some efforts for intrusion by, regional organisations. In the case of UNPROFOR, with significant contributions from NATO member states, and given the fact that the moves towards the disintegration of the Federal Republic of Yugoslavia were no doubt orchestrated by elements in some of the NATO member states, such intrusion was to be expected. Here again, I must compliment my senior military colleagues from the NATO fraternity, who kept me informed of the attempts at such intrusion so that the impact could be largely neutralised. This in many ways is a tribute to the military personnel who are deputed on UN missions, in terms of their commitment to the values enshrined in the UN charter. To that extent, I was lucky that in the year at the helm of the mission I did not have any stand-off with NATO. I do not think my successors were that fortunate.

The next problem relates to other UN agencies and international NGOs. This again needs to be managed with some understanding and finesse. My own experience with the late Mrs Sadako Ogata who was the United Nations High Commissioner for Refugees, and the International Committee of the Red Cross, was most rewarding. It lasted for years well beyond my UNPROFOR commitment. With Medicen Sans Frontieres (MSF), I had to handle the pressure generated on my Deputy Force Commander Philippe

Morillion; but stood by him without allowing their activities to impact the mission objectives.

And finally, permit me to comment on a point that has been made in the Concept Paper about UN PKO support for activities of international NGOs. I have severe reservations about this proposition because these NGOs have their own agenda to meet the aspirations of those who are funding them, and their objectives may not therefore always be in consonance with those of the UN Peacekeeping Mission. To that extent, it may be advisable to deal with this suggestion with some circumspection.

Challenges of Mission Leadership: Perspective of a former FC and Deputy SRSG (Deputy HoM) of UNMIS

Lt Gen JS Lidder, UYSM, AVSM (Retd)

The Environment

The past few years have witnessed widespread conflicts and violent environments across the world throwing new challenges for the international community. The entire UN system is outstretched - under scrutiny for its inadequacies, inaction and at places being controlled by certain powers. Notwithstanding, the world has been unable to produce alternate systems to replace the UN – specifically related to international peace and security.

New conflicts have added to unresolved disputes which the UN has been struggling to resolve for decades. These conflicts are hybrid in nature with heightened sectarian violence. Digital technologies and the inability of states to police their physical borders have given these conflicts a regional spread. The transforming nature of these conflicts has blurred the lines between conflict and post-conflict narratives - making conflict prevention, peace-making and peacebuilding all inclusive.

Geo-political competitiveness, proxy wars, internal strife, and cybercrime have aggregated the Covid-19 pandemic sufferings - unfolding grave human tragedy unseen since

World War II. Asymmetric and virus threats in particular have made safety and security a major concern in UN peace operations – particularly for troop-contributing countries (TCCs).

Ironically, the UN Security Council (UNSC), the legitimate organization to enforce international peace and security stands polarized – sending confusing messages to peacekeepers in the field. For UN missions to deliver in the developing ambiguity, leadership competence has become pivotal – demanding leaders and commanders to walk the extra mile for effective peacekeeping. Good leadership was the primary engine of the United Nations Mission in Sudan (UNMIS), in successfully implementing Sudan's Comprehensive Peace Agreement (CPA) from 2005-2011.

UNMIS Leadership in Sudan

I was honoured to be part of Sudan's peace process, resulting in the birth of South Sudan on 09 Jul 2011. During this period, I was Force Commander (FC) from Jan 2006 to April 2008 and Deputy Special Representative of Secretary-General (DSRSG-P) from Jan 2010 to Dec 2011. Sudan's civil war between the Government of Sudan (GoS) and Sudan's People Liberation Movement/Army (SPLM/A) had ended with the signing of the Comprehensive Peace Agreement (CPA) in Nairobi in 2005. UNMIS was established in 2006 through UNSCR 1590 (2005), to support the implementation of CPA, with an authorized strength of 10, 000 troops.

UNMIS Senior Mission Leadership (SML) worked as an integrated team - rising above turfs, silos, and egos. CPA was identified as central to mission mandate - for which all plans and resources got channelized. Institutionalised cooperation was evolved with a range of international and regional partners - to promote political dialogue, ethnic reconciliation, and shared conflict resolution strategies. Context is the key for each conflict intervention - and the tendency of senior leaders to template past mission experiences needs to be resisted.

The Special Representative of the Secretary-General (SRSG) and FC have a concurrent dual role – implementation of the mandate and managing the mission. Leading multinational and multidimensional representation in a violent zone is demanding, for which senior leaders need to be competently selected, and groomed for risk, opportunity, and balanced decision-making. FC's ability to operationally lead is prudent – delegating administration and management tasks to competent staff. There is a tendency in the UN secretariat to micromanage field missions, which is rightly resisted by upright SRSGs and FCs.

Civil-military collaboration is the foundation for mission success – yet tensions between civil and uniformed personnel many a time hamper joint planning and execution. The Senior Mission Leaders (SML) guide and synergize work between heads of office (HOO) and sector commanders (SC). There were aberrations - which were corrected with due diligence. Integration lies in the mind, I have therefore encouraged relationship building, so that the spirit behind joint working is well understood and respected.

The host nation must be on board, with state ownership where feasible. Established dialogue through joint structures and procedures greatly helps in the consensual progression of the peace process. Missions get their legitimacy (legality) through the mandate, but professional credibility can only be achieved through performance and outcomes. Earnest effort was made to build trust with local administrators and civil populations - which not only assisted in progressing the CPA smoothly but helped resolve daily functional issues of freedom of movement and diplomatic/custom clearances.

Digital technologies, especially communication and surveillance devices are being perceived as intrusive by many countries. Transparent whole-of-government and civil society engagement are necessary to convince them of governance's technological advantage. There are no easy answers to bringing human rights accountability to those in power. It requires building bridges and professional integrity to stand up to what is right.

Mandates - Formulation, Review, and Operationalization

UN mandates have become demanding and prescriptive – leading to bureaucratic tick-box responses in the field. There is a need for UNSC to enlarge consultation and crank TCCs into the strategic loop. Grounded conflict analysis is necessary to draw holistic mandates with a visionary end-state. Means must support mandates, as Kofi Annan famously said. I believe TCCs need to gradually start 'owning the mandates', as they get to operate beyond the standard peacekeeping envelope, to accept casualties.

The implementation of CPA required political partnerships and joint resolution of local conflicts. With multiple international players in the field, gaining consensus and assistance in mediation becomes desirable. But it can get in muddy waters. Political overlap in the handling of Abyei between the UN and African Union (AU) left the conflict unresolved - with the compromised establishment of the United Nations Interim Stabilization Force for Abyei (UNISFA) - an example of UN politics buckling under regional expediency.

Mission leadership faces a dilemma in interacting with local populations who are not a party to formal agreements. In Darfur and Abyei, Khartoum's narrative frequently conflicted with ethnic or cultural feedback and required ground verification. I flew ICC indicted Ahmed Haroun, the

Wali (governor) of Southern Kordofan to Abyei in 2010, to interact with Misseriya tribal leadership. The decision was questioned by many in the international community and media - but UNMIS's preventive diplomacy greatly helped to diffuse tensions. Importantly, it reinforced the UN's impartial sincerity in reaching out to multiple voices for peace in Sudan.

Digital technologies form an important tool for contemporary leadership – to understand, monitor, and adapt. However, technology is in support, and at no time should inhibit a leader's horse-sense to decide. As peace operations get kinetic, the balance between political primacy and delegated military authority should be well understood. I have strongly encouraged joint civil-military planning and ground interventions, which encourage transparency and coherence in-ground assessments.

The use of force is driven by international humanitarian and human rights laws, with minimum collateral damage. Militaries have to respect their strategic obligation to the political end state so that their operational activity contributes toward long-term stability. Concurrently, political leadership should recognize FC's decentralized control in operations. The military, in many missions, continues to be employed on a 'required-add-on' basis, which does not keep it sufficiently updated on political developments and humanitarian processes. Mainstreaming the military into a complete spectrum of mandated activity is essential so that troops are prepared and rehearsed to provide credible responses when crises occur.

The manoeuvre, both physical and mental, is the key to effective peacekeeping. All warfare is based on control of space, which implies a combination of pivots (operating bases) and manoeuvres (mobility platforms). To sustain control of far-flung areas, UNMIS pioneered the concept of 'Temporary Operating Base' (TOB) – a need-based temporary deployment. With increasing attacks on the UN, operating bases and facilities need to be protected against physical and standoff attacks - but fortressing is not the answer. While technology could assist in surveillance and protection, physical domination through deterrence patrols is an operational necessity.

While visiting the African Mission in Sudan (AMIS) in Darfur in 2006, I noticed a few bases being targeted by stand-off fire every night. The reason was simple - there was no outside movement after sunset. We made contingents start night patrolling, to start with close to the perimeter, and subsequently expanding outwards in concentric circles. When I revisited these units, I happily learned of a distinct reduction in fire assaults. The sheer churning noise and light glares of Armoured Personnel Carriers (APCs) appeared to have reduced rebel attacks considerably.

The overarching success story of Sudan has been the redeployment of SAF and SPLA across Line 1/1/56 – which was monitored through an elaborate network of ceasefire monitoring structures. I chaired Ceasefire Joint Monitoring Committee (CJMC), while SCs staffed Area Joint Monitoring Committees (AJMCs). For impartial jurisdiction, it was essential that CJMC got built into a professional team. A number of structural, procedural, and social initiatives, including the holding of retreats in Kenya, Uganda, and Egypt paid results.

As per CPA, CJMC was to meet fortnightly at Juba – which was turning into a theoretical conferencing exercise. We, therefore, decided to change this format and hold critical meetings at conflict spots. This was greatly appreciated by my Sudanese friends, who got a glimpse of hitherto inaccessible interiors, and the opportunity to interact with their ground commanders. It also gave us a true picture of the conflicts, at times different from reports.

Intense fighting broke out between SAF and SPLA in Malakal in November 2006, nearly leading to a relapse of war. 8 JAKLI under Colonel Bharat Shekhawat performed brilliantly by holding their ground, while the majority of UNMIS had evacuated. Seeing the criticality of the situation, I decided to fly to Malakal, with the airstrip under shelling. The CJMC met under fire over the next few days, supported by AJMC, to cease fighting. Once the fighting stopped, necessary support was provided for immediate mitigation. Malakal handling won widespread international recognition – but more importantly bolstered the image of UNMIS in both Khartoum and Juba.

Effective peacekeeping demands an operationally responsive logistics system. Habitat and equipment with low carbon footprint and environment-friendly technologies are the need of the hour. The Director of Mission Support (DMS) forms an integral part of SML, tasked to optimize finite resources – which are coordinated on a daily basis through the Mission Support Centre (MSC). The military must obtain helicopter mobility when operationally necessitated. Battle casualties have become a major concern for field missions. The UN has thus initiated major steps to reduce fatalities by upgrading medical support, which is turning out to be a confidence builder in combat.

Battlefield discipline is vital not only for operational success but also for survival. If a peacekeeper has no stomach for fighting, all he/she has to do is shirk, disobey, or lie. Well-commanded units rigorously follow their daily routine of training and administration, with sub-unit commanders participating. This not only helps to maintain a high degree of physical and mental fitness but keeps the troops motivated to deliver in adversity.

Empowering the TCCs

We appear to be obsessed with large troop numbers while planning peace operations. I have recommended quality over quantity. Fewer motivated troops, backed by force multipliers are a far better bet than a huge body mass with weak impact. I also believe that while homogeneity of national representation at the unit level is operationally desirable, mission deployments at the sector or regional level must reflect international heterogeneity. This cross-fertilizes global campaigning experience, as well as induces healthy, transparent competition between contingents.

Military contingents play a central role in contemporary peacekeeping, and need to bear this responsibility by shedding traditional peacekeeping mindsets. With the introduction of asymmetric and cyber threats, new technologies are being cranked in for operational effectiveness. New conflicts are undefined in space and time, while we continue to operate in the classical strategic-operational-tactical construct. Each action by a peacekeeper today is strategic in nature. This calls for a major attitudinal shift towards field delegation, where junior leaders are empowered to take time-critical decisions, without awaiting instructions from their superiors or national capitals.

Chain of command, caveats, gender, and accountability can become tricky ground, especially in high-tempo operations. We attempted to resolve these issues through strategic engagement with TCC permanent missions in New York, state capitals, and visiting dignitaries. Additionally, inter-sector dialogue was encouraged to infuse whole-of-mission military pride.

Protection of Civilians (POC)

Contemporary armed conflicts raise numerous issues regarding POC. The presence of UN peacekeepers not only generates global expectations but more importantly local aspirations, to protect vulnerable communities. The protection agenda has thus become central to UN peacekeeping. However, POC continues to be a sensitive leadership issue as mission performance is being judged primarily in the manner it protects civilians.

POC requires a collective effort, including international organizations, peace operations, and the humanitarian community. POC is a state subject. However, UN missions are mandated to assist the national authorities with a spectrum of responses 'up to and including deadly force', when the host nation is unable or unwilling to shoulder its responsibility. The situation has got repeatedly sensitive during physical interventions in South Sudan, as in a few other missions – putting UN's principles of 'consent' and 'use of force' under scrutiny.

UN DPO POC Policy 2019 is the basic guidance document. It recommends POC implementation in three tiers – protection through dialogue and engagement, provision of physical protection, and establishment of a protective environment. I have noticed a tendency of many to see these tiers as sequential. These tiers are inclusive and demand complementary use of resources adopting a comprehensive approach.

The four-phased POC activity (prevention, pre-emption, response, and consolidation) is neither linear nor a template for POC. Threat analysis and risk assessment lie at the heart of protection, requiring real-time information sharing and early warning. Joint Operations Centre (JOC) and Joint Mission Analysis Centre (JMAC) are the integrated mission structures to be contextualized for POC effectiveness. Technology is enabling missions to establish an all-weather vigilance grid, to operationalize POC scenarios with the mantra 'Predict and Prevent'.

UNMIS was amongst the first to formulate Mission POC Strategy, providing a strategic vision and defining roles and responsibilities for mission components. The POC concept envisaged task forces for different facets of POC. Civil affairs took the lead in political dialogue and local mediation - while the military led in physical protection. The lead player needs to be kept flexible depending upon the protection context.

Civilians and communities in the conflict zone are the main stakeholders – which are often forgotten. Community and tribal leaders can play a constructive role in the planning and coordination of protection efforts, for which there is a need to build trust. Women's representation and language competence need further emphasis in the militaries for effective networking with civil society.

Women continue to be impacted disproportionately in conflicts - ranging from death, injury, and displacement to sexual victimization. Gender mainstreamed approach is our collective tool for conflict management and post-conflict nation-building with women groups being incorporated in the entire spectrum of the conflict cycle. I found women's competencies at par when given latitude in responsibility.

With increased targeting of the humanitarian community, there is an opportunity for closer military-humanitarian collaboration with due accommodation for 'humanitarian space'. Humanitarian synergy was the essence of my leadership thrust as the UN head at Juba from 2010-to 11 - which helped to accelerate peacebuilding activities.

Strategic Communications

We live in an information age where strategic communications are becoming an inextricable part of peace operations – for credible messaging and managing expectations. All leaders need to be educated and trained in public information (PI) skills. UNMIS was posted with industrious PI staff who established a good interface with international and local media – using topical briefings and proactive press releases. The local press was identified as our primary audience with national staff harmonizing cultural and language sensitivity.

UN Juba Radio Miraya was used as a PI force multiplier for interviews, panel discussions, and community engagement. Effective use was made by me as Chairman CJMC to update the local population on conflicts, redeployment of forces, and POC with Sudanese Generals commenting alongside. In an information-void environment where rumours fly with ease, these briefings portrayed authentic updates.

Social media has become an unavoidable part of our lives for which the UN has issued detailed guidelines. Though the contemporary relevance of social media is indisputable, disinformation and weaponization of information are posing fresh challenges to peacekeepers. Cyber resilience training is therefore being administered on an urgent basis.

Training for Leadership

The success of a peace operation is largely dependent on the capability of peacekeepers and leaders to deliver in the challenging volatile environment. Standardized comprehensive training, both pre-deployment, and in-mission are now at the heart of the UN effort – with national and regional peace training centers interlinked.

The thrust of training should be on honing conflict-specific leadership skills and innovative joint operating techniques. With the hybridization of conflict environments, it is necessary that militaries train for high-intensity peace operations in an environment of ambiguity with the objective of countering unconventional and unpredictable threats with minimum losses.

I believe the concept of in-mission training needs to be further enlarged and made a function of command. TCCs should realize that such training is for their good, to reorient their concepts and battle drills for contextual operational effect. Each mission should be able to construct a combat training school that allows facilities for manoeuvred tactical training and firing of weapons, amongst others.

Effective peacekeeping is all about leadership. We need to select and train leaders who are qualified to handle new conflicts and lead in risk-prone areas. 'Comprehensive accountability' is the key, both for mandate evolution, delivery and conduct.

Challenges of Mission Leadership: Perspective of a former FC of MONUSCO

Lt Gen Chander Prakash, SM, VSM (Retd)

Introduction

United Nations is an organisation with the mechanisms necessary for dealing with developing humanitarian crisis situations and deteriorating security situations around the globe. Peacekeeping is effective at resolving civil wars, reducing violence during wars, preventing wars from recurring, and rebuilding state institutions. After the Cold War ended, there has been an increase in the number of peacekeeping operations. Post the end of the Cold War; the UN attempted to end 16 civil wars by deploying peacekeeping missions. Of those 16 missions, 11 missions can be said to have successfully achieved their mandate as these 11 countries where the UN peacekeeping missions were deployed did not return to civil war. The failure of the balance five missions could be said to be due to the UN's institutional shortcomings. Rwanda and Bosnia are examples of these.

Today's peacekeeping is expected to facilitate the political process, protect civilians, assist in the disarmament, demobilization, and reintegration of former combatants, support the organization of elections, protect and promote human rights and assist in restoring the rule of law.

Peacekeeping is a highly dynamic activity wherein the mission leadership faces a myriad of challenges in executing the mandate. The Centre for Creative Leadership has carried out a study to identify what is most challenging about leading organizations? The study found that leaders around the globe consistently face the same top six challenges. Challenges identified by this study are - honing effectiveness, inspiring others, coaching and mentoring effectively, leading a team which includes team building, team development, and team management, guiding a change, and managing stakeholders.[1] The mission leaders in a UN peacekeeping mission face plus some additional challenges that are peculiar to the environment in which they function.

Core Functions of UN Peacekeeping Mission Leadership

Contemporary peace operations are multidimensional, complex, dynamic, and demanding. Leadership in the UN peacekeeping operations is about performance both at the individual and organisational levels so as to accomplish the laid down objectives and achieve the desired impact and end results. In peacekeeping wherein, the host country is facing intrastate conflict and is in the process of transition from conflict to peace, the three core functions are: -[2]

(a) Create a secure and stable environment while strengthening the State's ability to provide security with full respect for rule of law and human rights.

---

1   Centre for Leadership, "The Top 6 Leadership Challenges Around the World", 24 November 2020, available at https://www.ccl.org/articles/leading-effectively-articles/top-6-leadership-challenges/, accessed on 15 May 2022.

2   Cedric de Coning, Julian Detzel, Petter Hojem, "UN Peacekeeping Operations Capstone Doctrine", NUPI seminar Report, 15 May 2008, available athttps://www.unocha.org/sites/dms/Documents/DPKO%20Capstone%20doctrine%20(2008).pdf, accessed on 10 May 2022.

(b) Facilitate the political process by providing dialogue and reconciliation.

(c) Supporting legitimate and effective institutions of governance.

(d) Provide a framework for ensuring that all UN and other international actors pursue their activities at the country level in a coherent and coordinated manner.

Leadership Framework

The UN based on the experience gained over decades has laid down a leadership framework that has eight defining characteristics that serve as guidelines in the selection of mission leaders and guide their functioning in the missions. These are enumerated below: -[3]

(a) **Norm Based.** In that it is grounded in UN norms and standards, beginning with the UN Charter.

(b) **Has to be Principled.** Mission leaders are expected to defend UN norms and standards and their application without discrimination, fear, or favour, especially in the face of pressure and pushback from powerful actors.

(c) **Inclusive.** Implying that the leaders must consider diversity as a strength, practice cultural and gender sensitivity and reject discrimination in all its forms.

(d) **Accountability.** Leaders at all levels are accountable both mutually within the UN system and to the beneficiaries/population of the host country.

---

3   UN System Chief Executives Board for Coordination, 'United Nations system leadership framework', 31 January 2018, available at https://unsceb.org/united-nations-system-leadership-framework, accessed on 15 April 2022.

(e) **Multidimensional.** It is expected that a leader will function in an integrated manner and engage with other pillars of the mission to achieve the larger objective.

(f) **Transformational.** Leaders should be able to bring about a positive change.

(g) **Collaborative.** There is a need to collaborate both within and outside the UN system for a leader to achieve the core objectives.

(h) **Self Applied.** The mission leaders are expected to act in accordance with UN principles and values and they must be self-motivated to do so.

Mission Leadership Team

UN Security Council mandates today are broader and more demanding than in the early days of peacekeeping. Peacemaking, peacekeeping, peace enforcement, and peacebuilding are now to be undertaken simultaneously. The differentiating lines between these are blurred. These must be mutually supportive as is the case in the United Nations Organization Stabilization Mission in the Democratic Republic of the Congo (MONUSCO). The nature of conflict continuously evolving, and its shades keep changing, hence the challenges, surprises, and frictions are continuously emerging. Mission leaders must be accordingly prepared to tackle and overcome these as a team, in a collaborative and integrated manner.

MONUSCO is an integrated and multidimensional mission that is led by the Special Representative of the UN Secretary-General (SRSG), who is the Head of the Mission. This core team consists of the Deputy SRSG (Rule of Law); the Deputy SRSG-Resident Coordinator/Humanitarian Coordinator (DSRSG-RC/HC); the Force Commander

(FC), the Police Commissioner (PC); the Director or Chief of Mission Support; and the mission's Chief of Staff. It also has Human Rights, Gender, Public Relations and Security heads as part of the Mission Leadership Team (MLT). Each of these components has an important role to play in the implementation of the mandate. Coordination among the various components is a challenge. MONUSCO being a laboratory of UN peacekeeping has effectively evolved a system in the form of the Joint Operation Centre (JOC) and Joint Mission Analysis Centre (JMAC) for better coordination and control within the mission.

Challenges of Mission Leadership

MONUSCO has complex mandates and unpredictable political support which has inherent challenges in implementation. It becomes more complex as the security situation does not guarantee the safety of UN peacekeepers and also their property. Some of the challenges faced by the mission leadership are discussed below: -

(a) **Mandates.** Mandates are political and diplomatic documents that have grown in size and tasking. In the case of MONUSCO, the mandate includes the protection of civilians, stabilization/nation-building tasks, and peace enforcement. It is a mission under Chapter VII with an unprecedented robust mandate. It is a challenge to successfully undertake all the listed tasks in the mandate simultaneously when there is no peace to keep, with limited resources placed at the mission's disposal, particularly with respect to the number of uniformed peacekeepers, mobility means, and logistic support. So far, there are no clearly defined exit guidelines.

(b) **Integration when there is No Peace to Keep**. In the eastern Democratic Republic of the Congo, because of the large number of armed groups operating in the area, the security situation is volatile. Some of the armed groups receive covert and tacit support from the DRC's neighbours. When there is hardly any peace to keep, integration of humanitarian and development partners creates difficulties for the partners, particularly if they are perceived to be too closely linked to the political and security objectives of the peacekeeping mission. Some of the partners feel that their too close integration with the peacekeeping mission hinders their effective functioning and also endangers their operations and the lives of their personnel. Advance planning including contingency planning with good internal communications has greatly helped in addressing this challenge. MONUSCO has adopted an Integrated Mission Planning Process (IMPP) that is intended to help all stakeholders of the UN system operating in the DRC arrive at a common understanding of its strategic objectives.

(c) **Training of Peacekeepers, Motivation, and Inter-operability**. The standard of training of peacekeepers greatly varies from one TCC to another and within a TCC from one contingent to the other. A lot depends on the guidance and directions the national contingent commanders receive from their capitals. Hence, it is extremely important to involve the TCC and contributing Member States in mandate formulation. Also, there are interoperability issues, particularly when the armed group activity extends to the boundaries of the two different TCCs areas of responsibility. Force Commander (FC)/Special Representative of the Secretary-General (SRSG) need to put in considerable effort to take on board the

Contingent Commanders and appeal to their good sense to deliver in case of a crisis situation. While some peacekeepers are self-motivated, some others are not. Risk aversion needs to be overcome by the FC/Deputy FC by setting a personal example.

(d) **Lack of Intelligence.** There is plenty of information available about many actors in a peacekeeping mission. Unfortunately, the information flow is not real-time and actionable. The induction of UAVs in MONUSCO is a welcome step as it has improved both the situational awareness and safety and security of peacekeepers. However, it is no substitute for human intelligence, which has its own challenges. For this, the mission leaders have to build faith and credibility with the civilian population and the host government authorities.

(e) **Coordination between Civil-Military Component of the Mission.** The civilian and military components tend to interpret a given situation differently. The civilian personnel of the mission area, are in the mission for a longer period than the uniformed peacekeepers. Though this is their strength, but they do not have full knowledge of how the militaries operate and their ethos. In a crisis situation, some civilian elements tend to exaggerate an adverse situation and place impractical demands on the uniformed peacekeepers. While on the other hand at times contingents tend to underplay the same. Getting to know the factual position and dealing with appropriately is a constant challenge for the HOM and the FC. Since the SRSG in MONUSCO (2011-2013) was well versed in military matters, friction and inertia between these two important components of the mission could be overcome. It will be useful if the civilian peacekeepers are educated on how the military peacekeepers operate, and their strengths and challenges.

(f) **Memorandum of Understanding (MoU).** In the case of missions like MONUC/MONUSCO which have been in existence for a long time, the MoUs are not updated/revised. Both for the TCCs and the administrative staff of the mission, the MoUs have financial implications. Thus, in military operations where flexibility is required to logistically support the operations, these become a restraining factor for the military leadership in the conduct of operations.

(g) **Disarmament, Demobilization, Repatriation, Reintegration and Resettlement (DDRRR) and Security Sector Reforms.** Disarmament, Demobilization, Repatriation and Reintegration (DDRR)/DDRRR are important mandated tasks for a peacekeeping mission. Unfortunately, adequate resources and schemes are not in place so that the surrendered elements of the armed groups can be reintegrated into society and earn a decent living. Consequently, they get recycled back to the armed groups. It is a challenge for the mission leadership to get the host government to take full ownership of this important mandated task as they have societal and financial challenges in this regard.

(h) **Inputs from NGOs and Humanitarian Teams.** NGOs and humanitarian actors operating in the mission area do a great job of alleviating the miseries of the local population and have an excellent rapport with the civilian population in the area. They can provide valuable information to the peacekeepers but for some reason, they tend to report developing adverse situations to their higher authorities before they share the inputs with peacekeepers locally. Then it is too late, and the media makes much of it and portrays it as a failure on the part of the mission.

(i) **Social Media.** Of late, there has been a proliferation of social media and smart phones in countries going through conflict situations. These are used to spread misinformation and misguide the local populace and incite them against the peacekeepers. Missions tend to be behind the curve; the result being violence against the UN peacekeepers and damage to UN property and assets. This is a challenge that has to be overcome in real-time. For this, the mission must work out a proactive strategic communication strategy and plan which is truthful, credible, and addresses all stakeholders, both nationally and internationally.

Conclusion

Based on the experience gained over several decades, the United Nations Department of Peacekeeping put in place processes and laid down norms so that they can select and depute leaders with high calibre and motivation for the missions; and it is bearing results. There are many imponderables and situations that leaders encounter on the job. Some do well in handling crisis situations and others may not do so for reasons mostly beyond their control.

Senior leadership in particular the SRSG and the FC have to deal with the host government and their Headquarters in New York. Mission leadership being at the operational level has to achieve the mission's core objectives as mentioned in this paper. They act as a bridge between the strategic (UN Headquarters) and tactical levels (ground realities). In an ever-changing politico-security environment there is a variation in interpretation of the mandate, directions, and guidelines. To be a part of the mission leadership in a challenging environment is something to be proud of. If things go well, it is very rewarding and self-satisfying, and if they don't - it is tough, lonely, and thankless. When there is genuine interest in the people, and mission leaders wish to secure and serve them well, they have to take risks and cannot be run-of-the-mill leaders. For a Force Commander in the UN, while it is about collaboration, courage, and risk, it is also about caution – "*do no harm*", especially when 'use of force' is needed to protect civilians.

Challenges of Mission Leadership: Perspective of Dy HoM and Director of Political and Civil Affairs of UNIFIL

Jack Christofides

Introduction

Leadership in peace operations can be seen to play out in three main ways. Firstly, mission leaders are responsible for guiding and supervising mission staff. Just in UNIFIL, there are approximately 11,100 people, including 800 civilians and 10,300 military staff. Secondly, mission leaders as heads of a UN body within the UN system apply their leadership in relation to UN Headquarters and to other UN bodies and entities within the UN system. Lastly, as senior UN officials, they must apply their leaderships vis a vis the outside world, in relation to the Member States, their nationals, the media, etc. In that role, they must be advocates, shapers of global narratives, and defenders of the UN Charter and of the reality on the ground.

The first responsibility, alone, is a formidable task. The UN workforce is one of the most diverse in the world and rotation rates among the military are high, with personnel deploying for a limited time – some troops for four months only – from all corners of the globe. They bring with them a wide range of expertise, profiles, backgrounds, and competencies. For mission leaders, maintaining cohesion and productivity, while steering the mission in choppy political and/or security waters, presents unique and difficult challenges.

UNIFIL is an interesting case among UN peace operations in part because of its unique leadership structure - a reflection of attempts to overcome the challenges of military-civilian cooperation within the mission. It is the biggest mission of the UN system by a large margin to be led by a military Head of Mission. The establishment of the civilian/substantive Deputy Head of Mission and the Principal Coordination Officer roles has sought to foster unity among the military, substantive, and support pillars of the mission and increase cohesion. In leadership, structure - not only personality - is crucial, and flexibility is key to striking a balance necessary for the good conduct of operations. During my time in UNIFIL, I have had ample opportunities to experience the power of complementarity and the balance between military and political leadership. While many aspects of mission leadership are common also in other contexts, I have chosen here to focus on the lesser-known ways in which leadership plays out in peace operations.

Designated Official

Besides their traditional leadership roles, heads of peace operations also hold the responsibility of Designated Officials in the country in which they are based. This role, which is perhaps less publicly known but nevertheless entails a heavy burden, means that they are responsible and accountable for the safety and security of all UN staff, including those who are members of UN agencies, funds, and programs. Given the spate of attacks against UN personnel and assets throughout the world, as well as exposure to other risks often associated with deployment in difficult environments such as transport accidents, natural disasters, or health, this is a grave responsibility with significant legal and moral implications.

As a Designated Official, the Head of Mission reports to the Under Secretary-General for Safety and Security, who is supported by the Department of Safety and Security in New York.

The Designated Official holds regular security management meetings with key personnel from the peace operation, security personnel, and representatives of UN agencies, funds, and programs. While significant latitude is given to a Designated Official, the prerogative to order an evacuation is retained by the Secretary-General. It is used rarely, given the obvious political and security implications of withdrawing UN staff and personnel from a country.

Headquarters

The most important relationship between the mission leadership and Headquarters occurs with the Department of Peace Operations. While all Heads of Mission are appointed by the Secretary-General, they work through the Under Secretary-General for Peace Operations. Official information about situational and operational developments on the ground is conveyed via code cables. Code Cables are the most formal communication between a mission and Headquarters and are always addressed to the Under Secretary-General for Peace Operations. In addition to establishing a narrative, cables also afford the Head of Mission the opportunity to make recommendations relating to policy.

Less formal, but no less important, means of communication are through VTCs, email, and, increasingly WhatsApp. There are obvious challenges using these less secure means of communications, but they allow an immediacy and interaction to communications that is not replicated through the more formal code cables.

In-person engagement is also very important. Senior leaders at UN Headquarters typically make several visits to the mission during their appointment, while mission leaders travel to New York every few months. Unfortunately, budget restrictions in recent years, not to mention the pandemic, have limited such travels.

In addition to the Under Secretary-General for Peace Operations, other key interlocutors for a mission are the Department of Operational Support, the Military and Police Advisers, and the regional desks. The bulk of communications between peace operations and Headquarters is in fact conducted through regional desks, which, as the name suggests, are arranged geographically. Each regional division is led by a Director who is the equivalent of a Major General.

Since 2019, there has been an important change to the way peace operations are run. The Secretary-General has delegated a great deal of authority for financial, personnel, and other administrative matters to the Head of Mission. The budget of peace operations can run into the hundreds of millions of dollars and the ability to shape the mission budget and account for spending is a vital role for Heads of Mission while they remain accountable to the Secretary-General.

There is of course a challenge that new Heads of Mission, who have no prior UN experience, face when assuming all these responsibilities. The plethora of acronyms, administrative rules and procedures can be onerous on long-standing UN staff let alone outsiders who join at a senior level. While some training is being provided by Headquarters, the challenges should not be underestimated for new Heads of Mission. Nevertheless, the delegation of authority seems to be a very popular measure, giving senior mission leaders far greater latitude to spend money and hire staff in order to keep processes going for the successful implementation of any mandate.

Security Council and the Member States

The mission leaders' role with regard to the Secretary General's obligations to the Security Council is to oversee the implementation of the mandate, report on progress, and advocate for policies in line with the goals of the UN Charter and the reality on the ground. They must sometimes take courageous and unpopular stances to influence and shape the political narrative in the service of truth.

With a few exceptions, all peace operations are mandated by the Security Council and most operations report regularly to it through the Secretary-General. Several peace operations report quarterly while others report less frequently through written reports to the Council and with briefings.

The Security Council can also ask missions to report on a specific incident, especially during moments of crisis. The format of the briefing can be either open or closed consultations. In missions led by a Force Commander who is also the Head of Mission (such as UNIFIL), the briefer is the Under Secretary-General for Peace Operations. In missions led by a Special Representative, he or she will usually brief the Council themselves.

These briefings are an important opportunity for the head of mission to shape the narrative and inform Council members of key developments in their area of operations. The Council may also decide to issue a statement following the briefing.

In addition to these formal briefings, maintaining relations with key Council members and their embassies in-country is paramount. In UNIFIL, the HoM/FC briefs both, in Israel and Lebanon, the diplomats of these key embassies. Over the last decade or so, the Council has adopted a practice whereby a Council member (usually one of the permanent members) is the pen-holder of the resolution. The majority of resolutions are adopted by consensus which means that all Council members have the opportunity to define the work of the mission. In this process, mission leaders also have an important role to play.

In addition to briefing the Security Council, Heads of Mission also brief the Troop Contributing Countries in New York and in-country, as well as other key Member States (e.g. contract groups, regional organizations, etc).

Conclusion

As leaders in peace operations, there is an apparent contradiction between our primary role, which is of service to the United Nations and the world, and leadership in its traditional definition. International civil servants work on behalf of the Secretary-General to implement mandates received from UN bodies, principally in the case of peace operations, the Security Council. Through them, they report and are accountable to the Member States and the peoples of the world in the implementation of their collective policies and decisions.

The responsibility of mission leaders is not only to guide, but also to supervise, and inspire our civilian and military personnel. Our responsibility is also as defenders of the UN Charter, its goals and values, and our mandates, and, in acting as guarantors of the integrity of peace operations, as the "eyes and ears" of the international community on the ground. We owe it to the world to advocate for the truth and courageously shape policies in defence of the UN Charter and the greater good of humanity.

(The views expressed in this article are those of the author and do not necessarily reflect the views of the United Nations Secretariat).

Special Remarks

Reflections of a Force Commander: Multidimensional Peacekeeping

Lt Gen S Tinaikar, SM, VSM (Retd)

The United Nations came into existence post the horrors of the Second World War to save succeeding generations from the scourge of war. The organization has indeed faced challenges in preventing conflicts between States and in the post-cold war period within States, but its contribution to international peace and security through its brief history has undoubtedly been remarkable. It is unfortunate that wars and internal conflicts have continued to extract a toll on life and adversely impacted the livelihoods of innocent civilians - women, children, and the elderly, despite efforts of the largest and the most influential international organization. But through each crisis over its 70-year existence, the United Nations has been the conscience-keeper of the world, upholding its purposes and principles, mitigating the horrible effects of war, and providing relief and humanitarian assistance to the vulnerable and the most in need.

The UN has had its successes in preventive diplomacy, peacemaking, and peacekeeping, but has been unable to meet every expectations in matters related to its core purpose – the maintenance of international peace and security. However, it is to the organization's credit that it has continuously drawn lessons from its successes and shortfalls and has evolved with changing mandate demands. It continues to serve humanity with greater efficiency and urgency with each passing year. Concomitantly, peacekeeping has made huge strides rising to the challenge of maintaining peace and stability in States wrecked by violence in the post-cold war era. Mandates today are consultative and focused, peacekeepers are better equipped and trained, safety and security of peacekeepers have gained tremendous importance, accountability is demanded from every leader and there is a greater emphasis on collective efforts – of the host nation, the region, sub-region, development partners, humanitarian agencies, NGOs and the international community under the banner of *UN*. The Declaration of Shared Commitments and Action for Peacekeeping Initiative of the Secretary-General have charted the way ahead and have found acceptance among more than 150 member states.

It is to be appreciated that Security Council mandates are defined by respect for the independence, sovereignty, and territorial integrity of each member state. Close partnership with the host nation, based on trust and fulfilment of common goals is mandatory for the success of a Mission. Moreover, peacekeeping is done following three inviolable principles: consent of parties, impartiality, and non-use of force except in self-defence and defence of the mandate. Operating under these conditionalities is a challenge when dealing with intra-state conflicts through multi-dimensional missions. Political, economic, and social fragility in host nations places civilians at risk of imminent violence and displacement. Signed Agreements often suffer from the vagaries of politics and implementation tends to lag, often in the face of violation. The element of uncertainty is real and apparent and can only be addressed through efforts of all partners acting in unison encouraging the host nation to abide by stated Agreements.

However, despite best efforts, the necessary political will is often seen to be absent and mission goals do get adversely impacted as a consequence. Consensus and unanimity so critical in politically charged environments fall short – a condition fraught with its own unique risks and dangers.

Between 1990 and 2013, the Security Council mandated 51 peacekeeping missions, 47 of which or 92% dealt with intra-State armed conflicts – a notable departure from the preceding 45 years, which witnessed only one such mission (ONUC – Congo) in the 60s. The five large multi-dimensional missions in Africa today are mandated to keep and build durable peace in States devastated by years of internal conflict. These States suffer from weak institutions, poor statesmanship, weak public finance management, and wealth distribution, lack of public space, and ill-trained uniformed and civil services all amidst abundant natural resources. In these challenging circumstances, missions aim to achieve a highly ambitious State Building agenda often in a politically divisive environment and with limited resources pegged against the urgency of time.

Protection of Civilians (POC) is the principal feature of every multi-dimensional mission. There can be no political and social advancement without "human security" in all its manifestations. Peacekeepers, military, and civilians are expected to employ all necessary means within capacity and areas of deployment, and the use of deadly force by the military is one of the tools available to protect civilians and advance the peace process.

POC, therefore, is a joint mission task, always guided by the political head of the Mission and heads of Field Offices. POC requires actions with both short and long-term outlooks based on analysis of the environment, the phase of the conflict, the mission's lifecycle, as well as the nature of the threat. It is strategized to be implemented in four phases: Prevention, Pre-emption, Response, and Consolidation. Pre-emptive deployment by military and civil components to mediate and reconcile warring groups or communities is essential. The involvement of local authorities through UN assistance provides a good foundation to mediate disputes and arrive at solutions. Concurrent development and peacebuilding initiatives to address root causes are vital to building durable peace.

Mandate delivery, therefore, is the "Whole of Mission" responsibility – not just of the Force. The Force can only provide physical security to civilians and UN personnel, installations, and equipment; one of the three tiers of the POC concept. The other two tiers are exclusive civil domains – Protection through dialogue and engagement and protection through establishment of a protective environment making it imperative for all mission pillars to act in unison. The Force guided by political leadership renders the best military advice on dealing with an explosive situation in the Mission Area. While the use of deadly force is always an option, the political implications of its use need to be understood and risk if any, accepted. Cooperation and understanding between all mission pillars, cultivated and nurtured assiduously, are mandatory for successful mission delivery.

The Force Commander (FC) exercises operational command and control over all uniformed personnel. But there are limitations to the authority of the FC, that need appreciation in multidimensional missions. Firstly, the tasking authority of "Enablers" – medical, engineering and aviation contingents is exercised by the Director/Chief of Mission Support (D/CMS), a civilian under the Department of Operational Support, responsible directly to the Head of Mission. Logistics, including the availability of arms, ammunition, and equipment of contingents is again entirely controlled by D/CMS, while administration and discipline of contingents and uniformed personnel is a national responsibility. Tasking of troops by the FC is again limited by provisions of the Status of Unit Requirement (SUR); the basis on which troop-contributing countries (TCCs) prepare, equip and deploy their contingents. Amendments to SUR are possible but must go through a long negotiation process and is time-consuming. The FC, aware of the variance of command and control responsibilities is required to provide the leadership and enthusiasm within the established parameters of Peacekeeping Command for the effective delivery of the Mandate. Building trust and confidence through the display of leadership skill and competency and presence at the critical location to guide and command contributes to success.

Diversity amongst contingents, in terms of language, military equipment, drills, and procedures can be overcome by providing separate and unique areas of responsibility. Operations by different contingents in a single region, such as the capital city example can also be addressed by further dissecting the region for distinctive tasking. The barrier of language is a major hindrance in translating a simple military command to action, particularly in dangerous situations.

There is adequate literature, policies, guidelines, and directives on almost every aspect of peacekeeping. It devolves on the FC to ensure that these are known, understood, and acknowledged by every contingent. The FC should also train and rehearse troops in contingency tasks, conducting tabletop and field exercises regularly. Should performance despite training and rehearsal be deficient on grounds of being risk-averse or other reasons, the FC is bound to report the same to the Office of Military Affairs at the UNHQ under information to the Head of Mission.

There does exist hesitation on the use of deadly force by peacekeepers which is not unreasonable. Mandates need to be achieved as far as possible without the use of force. The safety and security of peacekeepers should not be compromised. Should force be necessary for the defence of the mandate, it must be done so considering its political and security consequences after full consultation with the Head of Mission. The FC must ensure that Rules of Engagement are known to all subordinate commanders.

A healthy, cooperative relationship with the host government acknowledging and addressing differences that are bound to come up from time to time is extremely important. Should the Mission and the Host State find themselves regularly at odds, it builds a trust deficit affecting smooth mandate delivery and reflects on the Mission leadership too. Differences with the host government should be resolved with patience, skill, tact, and above all intelligence. An outright derogatory or condescending approach would further make the situation difficult and presents a reputational risk.

Finally, UN presence and operations must make a positive impact on the lives of the common people. The Mission cannot afford to lose the faith and support of the people they serve. Effective strategic communications ensure that the good work is known and recognized within the Mission Area and outside. It must be based on lived experiences, an improved security situation, greater freedoms, relief from humanitarian distress, and above all good governance and the rule of law.

Closing Remarks

Amb Vijay Thakur Singh

Today's discussions have been extremely informative and I do want to thank Lt Gen C Prakash for moderating the session. We would also like to thank Lt Gen Satish Nambiar, Lt Gen J S Lidder, Lt Gen S Tinalkar, and Mr Jack Christofides for joining in today's discussion. You bring great experience and great value to the topic we are discussing today.

ICWA and USI have been collaborating on a series of webinars and I would like to thank Maj Gen Goswami and Maj Gen Sharma for all the cooperation they have extended.

Today's webinar has been one of the best ones, as we are discussing issues on which the success of a mission depends, which is the leadership. The Challenges of Leadership in delivering the mandate are very critical when we discuss peacekeeping operations.

We do know that mandates have to be delivered and we do know that there is accountability. But there is also the fact that today the nature of peacekeeping has changed and it has become far more demanding, far more complex, and possibly more dangerous as well. This is because apart from inter-state conflict today we are also looking at intra-state conflict, which is far more difficult to handle.

This webinar is giving us an opportunity to assess the requirements, limitations, and challenges of mission leaders.

The conversation highlighted that the quality of leadership has to be of the highest calibre since as a mission leader one needs to deploy a range of skills, knowledge, and competence to work on the ground and deliver the mandate. It is a responsibility that requires great leadership qualities.

The second point which was highlighted by all the speakers was the importance of communication. As mentioned by Gen Nambiar, communication is needed with the UN Headquarters because this can support the functioning of missions. Communication with the UN Headquarters is also important since it provides an input into the decision-making, which apart from operational also takes strategic decisions. Another point was on the role of TCC which needs to be made far more active and their voices heard in decision-making at the UN.

The third point made in today's discussion was on the need for a consultative leadership at the ground level which gives a sense of being stakeholders to all the components of the mission. It is also equally important to have a good civil-military relationship on the ground. The next aspect is the need for communication with the local population since it is the local population that would determine how easy or difficult the job will be for the Mission Leader.

The other point mentioned was that since the composition of the peacekeeping is very diverse there is a need for skills and sensitivities in handling troops. Training and knowledge of the characteristics and cultural background of the troops contributing countries are required. Training is also required in terms of dealing with new challenges which today include the Protection of Civilians.

Last but not least is strategic communication. A number of players remain out in the field such as the press, NGOs, local population, etc for which communication is very important. We are using new technologies in order to reach out to various stakeholders. Technology is also important in providing better situational awareness and addressing strategic gaps while working on the ground. India has been pushing this forward and has recently launched a technology platform for peacekeepers called UNITE AWARE platform. The integration of technology is very useful for peacekeeping operations.

Finally, even though the nature of UN Peacekeeping has changed in the last six decades, there are three principles that remain integral and are the basis of the mandates of the UN Peacekeeping operations: one, consent of the parties; second, impartiality; and third, non-use of force except in self-defence and defence of the mandate. These three continue to be the guiding principles of UN Peacekeeping operations.

With this webinar, we come to the end of the six series of webinars on UN Peacekeeping. We look forward to continuing to work with USI on other projects in the year to come.

Thank you so much for your participation.

www.ingramcontent.com/pod-product-compliance
Lightning Source LLC
LaVergne TN
LVHW050930200726

843508LV00011B/2304